RUE ORDENER
RUE LABAT

RUE ORDENER
RUE LABAT

Sarah Kofman

Translated by Ann Smock

UNIVERSITY OF NEBRASKA PRESS

LINCOLN & LONDON

© Éditions Galilée, 1994
© 1996 by the University of Nebraska Press
All rights reserved
Manufactured the United States of America
⊗ The paper in this book meets the minimum re-
quirements of American National Standard for
Information Sciences – Permanence of Paper for
Printed Library Materials, ANSI Z39.48-1984
Set in Robert Slimbach's Adobe Minion
Typeset by Tseng Information Systems, Inc.
Book design by Richard Eckersley

Library of Congress
Cataloging-in-Publication Data
Kofman, Sarah.
[Rue Ordener, Rue Labat. English]
Rue Ordener, Rue Labat / Sarah Kofman;
translated by Ann Smock. p.   cm. – (Stages; v.7)
ISBN 0-8032-2731-0 (cloth: alkaline paper). –
ISBN 0-8032-7780-6 (paperback: alkaline paper)
1. Kofman, Sarah – Childhood and youth.
2. Jews – France – Biography. 3. Holocaust, Jewish
(1939–1945) – France – Personal narratives.
4. Holocaust survivors – France – Biography.
I. Title. II. Series: Stages (Series); v.7.
DS135.F9K644 1996
940.53'18'092–dc20 [B]
95-52462 CIP

SECOND PRINTING: 1997

CONTENTS

Sarah Kofman self-portrait 1991.
Courtesy of Ann Smock.

TRANSLATOR'S INTRODUCTION

Rue Ordener, Rue Labat turned out to be Sarah Kofman's next-to-last work. She was not quite sixty years old when she wrote it. Professor of philosophy at the Sorbonne, author of more than twenty books on philosophy, art, literature, and psychoanalysis, she was one of France's most important contemporary thinkers. Jean-Luc Nancy, Philippe Lacoue-Labarthe, and Jacques Derrida were among her allies, especially through the philosophy series, La Philosophie en effet, that they initiated together in the midseventies, and she maintained her ties with them despite differences in temperament and direction. She made a profound impression on her students and on their students and on the many young people who met her in the various parts of Europe and the Americas that she visited as a teacher and lecturer. She died by her own hand in October 1994.

Around New Year's Day 1993, she began writing *Rue Ordener, Rue Labat;* she finished the manuscript that autumn. It is an account of her childhood between the ages of eight and about eighteen: it begins on the last day she ever saw her father, 16 July 1942 — the day the Vichy police picked up the Rabbi Bereck Kofman in the family apartment on the Rue Ordener in Paris — and ends when she enrolled at the Sorbonne in the midfifties. On the opening page she suggests that it might be the book to which all her others had indirectly been leading her.

The day Bereck Kofman was picked up, thirteen thousand other Jews were taken too, in a single roundup. They were herded into the winter cycling arena, the Vélodrome d'Hiver, and then dispatched to a camp at Drancy to await deportation. Between the Armistice in 1940 and the Liberation in '44, some eighty thousand Jews residing in France were destroyed. The obligation to acknowledge this disaster has, in the last twenty years or so, become a painfully complicated national preoccupation in France. But at the end of the war, the catastrophe suffered by Jews was so far from being recognized by the victorious Resistance and the French population in general that Jews were urged, on occasion even by members of the Resistance, to be "discreet" about the persecution they had suffered and the property that had been stolen from them. They were warned of the new wave of anti-Semitism that they might provoke by indelicate candor. Indeed, there appeared in '44 and '45 a dozen associations for the protection of the rights of French citizens who had profited from Jewish losses. Such small-minded expressions of resentment against so-called privileged victims came from a minority of French men and women to be sure, and this hostility never seriously threatened the official guarantee of full civil rights for Jews made in August '44, but it contributed to the considerable hardships that many Jews experienced in their efforts simply to find a place to live and some means of support when they returned from the camps or, like Sarah Kofman's mother in the fall of 1944, came out of hiding.

By 1993 Sarah Kofman had already published four very brief autobiographical fragments, two of which, like *Rue Ordener, Rue Labat,* bear directly on memories of the war. Moreover, in 1987 she had dedicated *Paroles suffoquées* (Stifled words) to the memory of her father, killed at Auschwitz. That volume is dedicated to three people in all: to the author's father, to Robert Antelme, a survivor whose one book, *L'Espèce humaine* (1957), on the camps, she called sublime, and to Maurice Blanchot, a contemporary writer and thinker whose disparate, fragmentary reflections on the Holocaust impressed her profoundly. But the bulk of Sarah Kofman's writing is not directly related to the war. She wrote on Plato and Socrates, on Rousseau and Diderot, on Auguste Comte, on E. T. A. Hofmann. She is best known for her work on Nietzsche and on Freud: her study, that is, of each one through ideas gleaned from the other or, rather, the contest in which she pits them by turns each against the other. This match unfolded in a succession of books starting in 1970 with *The Childhood of Art* and came to a halt with the two thick volumes on Nietzsche's *Ecce Homo* published in 1992 and 1993, *Explosion I,* and *Explosion II. Rue Ordener, Rue Labat* is thus something of a departure in her oeuvre: for one thing, it is her only piece of sustained narrative writing.

Antelme said that, upon their return, survivors of the Nazi camps "were all seized by a veritable delirium. We wished to speak, to be heard at last. And yet, it was impossible. We had hardly begun to speak and we were choking." Blanchot has long emphasized the obligation to speak at such moments: when, that is, one lacks the power to do so. He means, I think, not only that certain situations require one to speak even though it is impossible, but also that they ask one to speak a language that power doesn't know. Speech, in its deepest dimension, is the way one responds to the obligation to preserve language, at least some of the time, from power—the power, notably, to grasp, comprehend, master. In the book she dedicated to Blanchot and Antelme and her father, Sarah Kofman acknowledges this duty to safeguard, by speaking, the limit at which something speaks that is other than power and other, even, than possibility.

During her life, she spoke and wrote a great deal; she worked fast, with verve and relish, which allowed her to overcome a great many obstacles. I admired the irreverent energy in her books—their high-spirited, Nietzschean malice. She was always deflating philosophy. She tracked "the question of women" in great works of the Western tradition right to the weak point or blind spot where the real stakes in the system are exposed. It made her jubilant, she said, to show how the greatest thinkers are led all unknowingly by the very drives and instincts from which they believe their thought to be utterly independent. She would not credit philosophy's solemn remove from art, either. She liked to play the role of the mocking girl whose laughter interrupts the philosopher at his desk, scatters his grave truths the better to greet in their stead beautiful

fictions, uncanny signs, and figures "devilishly deceptive."
That splendid mask of insolently feminine brilliance is
not apparent at all in *Rue Ordener, Rue Labat,* which, I
would say, does without literary qualities.

It is simple, but it does not have a simple style or any
style. You would not say of it "well written" or "a good
story." Fortunately, it exists and is plainly legible.

Unless I am mistaken, she began writing it with a sense
of unexpected renewal. There was an unanticipated opening in her thoughts. It seemed that rather suddenly she
was able to turn toward a sort of knot in her past, into
which her heart was tied, a knot formed during the war in
Paris on the Rue Labat, in the apartment where a Christian woman took her in on the night she and her mother
learned that the Gestapo was coming for them on the Rue
Ordener. This woman hid them both till the Liberation. It
was a treacherous rescue, a generous swindle.

Sarah Kofman was one of many Jewish children who
were entrusted during the war to non-Jewish households,
whose salvation required them to forsake the teachings of
their parents, whose emergency families sometimes did
not want to give them up when the real parents returned,
or whose parents, once back, were unable to care for
them, or whose parents never reappeared, and who, for
these or still other reasons, became the objects of painful disputes among adults with almost unbearably complicated motives or among differing agencies within the
drastically weakened Jewish community that sought to

take responsibility for the welfare and education of Jewish children in distress. Sarah Kofman might have compared memories with other Jews of her generation, I suppose, but though I could be wrong, I doubt that she ever did at any length before she wrote this book. Unexpectedly, she found that she could tell the story to a physician whom she consulted regularly (she was often ill), and she dedicated *Rue Ordener, Rue Labat* to him. So whereas in *Paroles suffoquées* she had to make a mute voice heard—a voice that was not just bereft of, but also preserved from, all ability and capability—in this more recent book it became possible after all to break an old silence.

Nonetheless, there is a similarity between the two volumes, and it is due, I think, to this one's being bathed in a lucidity unclouded by insight. No sense of understanding or ultimate resolution—no relief, no consolation whatsoever—mars it. It is clear.

Many of Sarah Kofman's works have been translated into English. Here is a partial list.

"Damned Food" and "Nightmare: At the Margins of Medieval Studies," both translated by Frances Bartkowski, in "Autobiographical Writings," an issue (number 49) of the review *SubStance*. These are the two autobiographical fragments bearing on memories of the war that I mention above.

The Childhood of Art: An Interpretation of Freud's Aesthetics, translated by Winifred Woodhull (New York: Columbia University Press, 1988). The original, *L'Enfance de l'art,* appeared in France in 1970.

Freud and Fiction, translated by Sarah Wykes (Boston: Northeastern University Press, 1991). The original was called *Quatre Romans analytiques* and appeared in France in 1974.

The Enigma of Woman: Woman in Freud's Writings, translated by Catherine Porter (Ithaca, N.Y.: Cornell University Press, 1985). *L'Enigme de la femme* came out in France in 1980.

Nietzsche and Metaphor, translated by Duncan Large (Stanford, Calif.: Stanford University Press, 1993). This volume includes a complete bibliography of Sarah Kofman's works, compiled by Duncan Large in consultation with Kofman. *Nietzsche et la métaphore* appeared in France in 1983.

The two volumes of *Explosion* are currently being translated by Duncan Large.

RUE ORDENER

RUE LABAT

for Philippe Cros

I

Of him all I have left is the fountain pen. I took it one day from my mother's purse, where she kept it along with some other souvenirs of my father. It is a kind of pen no longer made, the kind you have to fill with ink. I used it all through school. It "failed" me before I could bring myself to give it up. I still have it, patched up with Scotch tape; it is right in front of me on my desk and makes me write, write.

Maybe all my books have been the detours required to bring me to write about "that."

II

On *16 July 1942,* my father knew he was going
to be picked up. It had been rumored that a big
roundup was planned for that day. He was rabbi
of a small synagogue on the Rue Duc in the 18th
arrondissement. He had left home very early that
day to warn as many Jews as he could to go into
hiding immediately.

Then he came home and waited: he was afraid
that if he too were to hide his wife and six young
children would be taken in his place. He had
three girls and three boys between two and twelve
years old.

He waited and prayed to God that they would
come for him, as long as his wife and children
could be saved. In a corner of the room (my
father's room, the biggest and nicest of the apartment, the best furnished, paneled and papered,
mysterious, and invested with a sacred quality—
for my father carried out all kinds of religious
ceremonies there, marriages, divorces, circumci-
sions), I watched his every gesture, fascinated.
The memory of the sacrifice of Isaac (whose de-
piction in an illustrated Bible, my Hebrew text-

book from early childhood, had often worried me) fluttered through my mind.

Four in the afternoon. Someone knocks. My mother opens the door. A cop with an embarrassed smile asks, "Rabbi Bereck Kofman?"

"He isn't here," says my mother. "He's at the synagogue."

The cop doesn't insist. He gets ready to leave. Then my father comes out of the room where he'd been resting and says,

"Yes, I'm here. Take me!"

"You can't, I have a babe in arms who isn't two yet!" says my mother, showing him my brother Isaac. Then she adds,

"I'm expecting another baby!"

And she thrusts out her stomach.

My mother is lying! My brother had just turned two on 14 July. And she wasn't pregnant, as far as I knew! I couldn't be as certain on this point as on the first, but I felt very ill at ease. I didn't know yet what a "white lie" was (at that time they weren't taking fathers of children under two years old, so if the cop had believed my mother my father would have been saved), and I didn't understand very well what was happening: the idea that my mother could lie filled me with shame, and I said to myself, anxiously, that perhaps after all I was going to have another little brother.

The cop, for his part, looks embarrassed. He doesn't want to make a decision, so he asks my mother to come along to the police station with my father in order to straighten things out.

They leave.

We find ourselves in the street, all six of us, pressed close together, sobbing very hard and wailing.

When I first encountered in a Greek tragedy the lament "ô popoï, popoï, popoï," I couldn't keep myself from thinking of that scene from my childhood where six children, their father gone, could only sob breathlessly, knowing they would never see him again, "oh papa, papa, papa."

III

As it turned out, we never did see my father again. Or get any news of him, either, except a card sent from Drancy, written in purple ink, with a stamp on it bearing Marshal Pétain's picture. It was written in French in someone else's hand. Apparently he hadn't been allowed to write in Yiddish or Polish, the languages he ordinarily used with us. My parents had immigrated to France in 1929 and were not particularly assimilated; all of us children, born in France and naturalized French citizens, learned French at school. In that last sign of life we had from him, where he told us he was being deported, he asked that in the two-kilogram packages we were legally authorized to send we be sure to include cigarettes. And he asked my mother to take good care of the baby.

When my mother died, it wasn't possible to find that card, which I had reread so often and wanted to save. It was as if I had lost my father a second time. From then on nothing was left, not even that lone card that he hadn't even written.

After the war the death certificate arrived from Auschwitz. Other deportees returned. One Yom

Kippur, at the synagogue, one of them claims to have known my father at Auschwitz. According to him my father survived for a year. One day when he refused to work, a Jewish butcher-turned-Kapo (on returning from the death camp, he reopened his shop on the Rue des Rosiers) supposedly beat him to the ground with a pickax and buried him alive. It happened on the Sabbath: my father, according to the story, said that he had been doing no harm, only beseeching God for all of them, victims and murderers alike.

For that, my father along with so many others suffered this infinite violence: death at Auschwitz, the place where no eternal rest would or could ever be granted.

IV

"Most of all, send cigarettes, blue or green Gauloises." Cigarettes were one thing he couldn't do without. At home, as soon as the Sabbath was over, he would light one up. The rule against smoking on that day was especially hard on him. We would spend the last hours of the day together in his room singing Hebrew songs and others whose words he had made up himself; later I recognized one of the tunes in a symphony by Gustav Mahler.

We all marched around hand in hand as my father's room grew darker and darker, watching for the three stars whose appearance would put an end to his ordeal. Then he would light a twisted red candle, saying the kiddush with a glass of wine in his hand; then he extinguished the candle with the overturned glass and lit the electric lights. Then he would smoke.

During the war, when tobacco was rationed, I used to pick up cigarette butts for him on the sidewalk, and I liked to go to the Rue Jean-Robert and buy him the Zig-Zag paper he used to roll his cigarettes.

Later, in a dream, my father appeared to me as a drunk zigzagging across the street.

V

At home a religious atmosphere prevailed. My father was a rabbi, and we rigorously observed all the kosher prohibitions. We lived in terror of using the wrong plate or utensils or of inadvertently switching on the electricity on the Sabbath. In winter, a "goy" woman would come that day to light the stove and warm up the food that had been prepared the night before. It surprised me that she should have the right to do what was forbidden to us.

My father spent almost all his time at the synagogue, and we would join him there on Saturday and on holidays. It was located on the Place Jules-Joffrin, quite far away, two Métro stops from the Rue Ordener, and we had to go and come back by foot.

On the way back I often used to hold my father by the hand, and he would tell me, in Yiddish, with a nice, slightly satirical smile, to pick up my feet. We would pass in front of the big clock on La Chapelle Station, and I could always amaze everyone by guessing the exact time without looking, almost to the minute.

On Rosh Hashanah, which was also my birthday, we would listen to my father blow the shofar. My mother was very proud of him, insisting that he did it better than anyone else. He practiced at home, and I would see him take out the shofar and put it away again in the drawer of a wardrobe where he kept it next to his tallith, his phylacteries, and the razor with which he slaughtered chickens according to the ritual. Every Friday evening, women would wait in our entryway, their net bags laden with one or two chickens. I played ball against the wall and carefully watched my father's comings and goings from the bathroom to the waiting room. It was all very mysterious and filled me with alarm. I associated the shohet's razor with Abraham's knife and the guttural sounds of the shofar with cries from the chickens' severed throats.

On Yom Kippur, we would spend the whole day in the synagogue on the Rue Duc. My father presided over the fasting, and my two sisters and I played in the courtyard with the three Adler brothers. My parents were close friends of the Adlers, who lived on the Rue Simart. The father and mother and one of the daughters were deported and died. Later at the Sorbonne I ran into one of the brothers, Oscar, the one who was my age and who also studied philosophy. We met once again at a reception at Aubier's — it was very moving.

I loved Passover and all the preparations for it. My mother would cleanse the kitchen things, and I can still see her looking under the bed with a flashlight to make sure that not a single crumb of bread had eluded her. I was very scared when she opened the door to the landing to let in the Prophet Elijah, for whom a place had been saved at the seder table. I loved singing the traditional songs in Hebrew, listening to the recital of the seven plagues of Egypt and to the reasons my father gave to explain why we must eat bitter herbs and other special foods on that night. And great was my emotion and my pride when I had to answer the ritual questions directed to children during the seder. I was also very fond of Purim, when my mother would scare us by putting on horrible masks; of Simhath Torah, when we'd see my father dancing in the synagogue with other

Hasidim and lifting high the scrolls of the Torah, which we would all go up afterwards to kiss. And Sukkoth, when we would have our meals for several days in booths made of branches, specially constructed for the occasion in our entryway.

VI

After 16 July 1942, the roundups got worse: women, old men, children, Jews who were naturalized French citizens as well as those who were not — no one was spared anymore. School was out of the question, for fear we would be picked up. Anyone wearing the star was liable to be nabbed on the way home. My father had gone one day to the police station to get us those insignia, those signs of infamy; my mother had sewn them onto our coats. It was no longer just by our noses or circumcized genitals that we Yids could be recognized. "Starred" as we were, and packed into the last cars on the Métro in third class, we were becoming easier and easier to round up.

At recess at my school on the Rue Doudeau-ville, I was called a dirty Yid. One day I was surprised to see one of my playmates, Jeanne Le Sovoi, who was seven years old then like me, respond by giving the girl who insulted me a slap across the face. Later, after the war, I ran into her again when we were both in our last year at the Lycée Jules-Ferry. She was in applied science; I was in philosophy. We exchanged only a few words: it was all still too recent for me even to mention without starting to cry. But just a few years ago I met this Jeanne from my childhood once again by chance, and this time I was able to speak to her about the time she had proved so brave; she didn't even remember it!

However she did remember our distress at the beginning of the school year in October 1943, when we learned that Hélène Goldenberg, the top student in our class, had been deported. She was a Rumanian Jew; she lived on the Rue Emile-Duployé; she was caught in the huge roundup at the Vel d'Hiv, the cycle-racing arena, and never came back. Another sinister piece of news that October: Mathilde Klaperman had just died. Her mother, losing all hope, unable to bear her husband's deportation, had turned on the gas in the apartment during the night.

Our teacher told us about the tragedy in class. She was Madame Fagnard, in charge of the second year of the elementary program. Despite the prevailing anti-Semitism, she bravely urged her pupils to attend Mathilde Klaperman's burial.

I loved almost all the teachers at that primary

school on the Rue Doudeauville. Mademoiselle Chevrin, who had us sing on the playground: "In the woods every Sunday, the little birds. . . ." And also later, after the war, when I was able to go back to school, Mademoiselle Bordeaux. But Madame Fagnard I revered. She was not only a remarkable teacher but a thoroughly kind woman, sensitive to everyone's troubles.

Whenever the siren sounded, we would go down into the cellar of the Lemire bookstore with her. She made us forget about the air raid and our fright by having us sing or play games or by telling us stories like the rather disturbing *Pied Piper of Hamelin* to distract our attention from the immediate danger. She gave piano lessons in her home. Knowing my family's poverty, she didn't make me pay for the lessons. She would come to the house bringing us toys, stories from the Bicot series, and other books. I remember getting a little doll from her (the only one I wasn't afraid of), housed with its clothes in a small brown artificial snakeskin trunk. To my utter despair, I was never able to get it back after our apartment was sealed off by the police. But on the night I left to hide in the home of "the lady on Rue Labat," I did take along *The Misadventures of Jean-Paul Chopard,* an illustrated book in the "Pink Collection," which Madame Fagnard had given me for my birthday (I had gone to her apartment, at 75 or 77 Rue de La Chapelle, and right there on the doorstep I had said, "It's my birthday today!" And she had gone to find me a book. She knew from the number of books I borrowed from the school library that reading was my passion. I think I must have told her how when I read *Merlin the Magician* I got so absorbed that, tipping back in my chair, I fell into the fireplace without even noticing and calmly went on with my reading.).

Once in a while she would take my sisters and me sightseeing in Paris and the surrounding area: Mont Valérien or the zoo at Vincennes. The time we went to the zoo, each of us brought home a postcard of our own choosing: Rachel got the elephant, Annette the monkeys, and I the bear.

When food rationing started, she asked her pupils to bring carrots and potatoes to give to the old people of the neighborhood who were especially needy.

When she handed out dietetic cookies and skim milk in the school courtyard, she served me as much as I wanted, much more than the prescribed portions. One day during my last year, I drank so much milk at recess that I vomited in the middle of class. I was put in a corner, on my knees. This incident was all the more upsetting to me because my family had always forbidden me to kneel: it was much too Christian a posture.

When Jewish Communist organizations urged my mother to hide us in the countryside and furnished us with fake ration cards, we chose, for an alias, our teacher's name.

VII

So between July of '42 and February of '43, my
mother undertook to hide us. Isaac ("christened"
Jacquot) and Joseph, who were very young, were
put in a nursery school in northern France.
Annette, who had just had surgery for double
mastoiditis and whose health was fragile, was
cared for in Nonancourt, in Normandy south of
Rouen, by a Jewish Communist woman named
Jeannette, who was married to a Gentile. When
she learned of our situation she took it upon
herself to find peasants who could lodge some
young Parisians with nothing to eat (that was the
official reason). Rachel (transformed into Jacque-
line), Aaron (now Henri), and I were hidden a few
kilometers from Nonancourt, in Merville.

It was there I discovered the countryside, farm
animals, and peasant food, which was so different from the food of my childhood. School was
five kilometers away, and we went on foot. I had
a hard time, weighed down by heavy clogs and
stiff with chilblains. It was always good to arrive
for class at that one-room school. My teacher was
Madame Morin. I set off gales of laughter and

won the friendship of all my classmates by reciting *The Cockerel, the Cat, and the Mouseling* with an incredible lisp. School was the only place where I felt "myself." There, I could just manage to stand being separated from my mother. Otherwise I spent my time crying and refused to eat, especially pork, which had always been forbidden me. This refusal, whose pretext was obedience to my father's law, must also have served, without my being completely aware of it, as a means of returning to my mother. Indeed, my sister Rachel wrote to her that she would have to take me back, for my behavior threatened to make it obvious to everyone that we were Jews. It was decided I should return. In the dark of night I was taken back to Paris by Jeannette's sister, Edith (also a Jewish Communist).

Three in the morning: Edith is afraid to go to my mother's apartment; we may have been followed. She asks me whose house we could turn up at without warning so late at night. I couldn't think of anyone but Madame Fagnard. I can still see her surprised and worried face when she opened the door. She made no comment at all, only asking us not to make any noise so as not to wake her aged, infirm mother. She made me some herb tea, brought covers, and I went to sleep, exhausted, in one of her living room armchairs.

VIII

The real danger: separation from my mother. Sometime between the ages of two and three years old, I lost sight of her for a few moments in the garden of the Sacré-Coeur near the big reflecting pool, and I started to wail. At three and a half, when I was sent to a summer camp at Berck-Plage with my sister Rachel, who was seven, I couldn't leave her side for a second. I even followed her into the bathroom, and she was obliged to play and swim with the toddlers because she had to stay with me. One day, in a wood where we were playing a game of tag, my sister got the handkerchief and started to run. I thought she was leaving, and I ran after her. Exasperated, the counselor picked me up, carried me far from the game, and left me alone despite my wailing. I fainted and woke up in the infirmary. There I stayed, sick, for the several days left until my return home.

The Gare du Nord: glued to the train window, I watch for my parents and at last catch sight of my father's smile. I am saved. After this episode my character changed. I became irritable and whiny and sucked my thumb incessantly.

When I came back from Merville, I stayed home with my mother. Since I was no longer going to school, I became a schoolteacher myself and taught my mother to read and write in French (with the help of the textbook *Antoine and Antoinette,* which I had kept). We also knitted together with scraggly yarn. Once more, just as when I had the mumps and couldn't go to school for forty days, I had my mother all to myself for whole days at a stretch.

From time to time, friends, wives of other deportees, came to visit us. One of them told how she had got "news" of her husband by going to consult a fortuneteller. We also went to the Rue des Charbonniers to read the tarot cards. The seer —clairvoyant!— declared that a great danger was threatening my father. She saw him surrounded by flames and also saw tall, smoking chimneys. When we walked out the door onto the Boulevard Ornano, my mother and I were not exactly reassured! We were convinced the occult sciences had a great deal to tell about the fate of those who had disappeared and who sent no news.

IX

The roundups got still worse, and my mother was afraid to keep me with her. Again she tried to hide me. First, in the country, in Picardy. I stayed there two days, crying and refusing to eat. My mother took me back again and decided to hide me in Paris, where she could come to see me more easily. I was taken in by quite a nice family on the Rue du Département. They let me look at their many books. I lasted one week. I was also hidden at the Claude-Bernard Hospital in the contagious ward — quarantined, as if I had scarlet fever. The nurses had me roll up balls of yarn and kept me going on comic books: I read *Bibi Fricotin* and *Les Pieds Nickelés,* which enabled me to hold out for three days. Then I was a boarder in a house on the Rue des Petits-Ménages, where I discovered dormitories and rutabagas and waited impatiently for my mother's visits; she brought me gingerbread that she'd made herself with fructose. I hoped more than anything that she would come to take me back, and once again, I refused to eat pork.

The only thing left was to hide me in a shelter

for Jewish children where I could continue to eat kosher.

We went to the Rue Lamarck. I had the hiccups and vomited when we got there. My mother attended to the administrative formalities and left. In the stairway she heard me weeping, crying, wailing. She turned around and came back, and this time I left with her.

During the following night, the Gestapo came to the Rue Lamarck, and the Jewish children were all deported. My mother proclaimed it a miracle and resolved to keep me with her from then on, no matter what happened.

"It" was not long in happening.

9 (?) February 1943, eight in the evening. We are in the kitchen having some vegetable broth. There is a knock. A man enters: "Go into hiding immediately with your six children. You are on the list for tonight." And he hurried away.

I never saw him again.

Whenever there were rumors of a roundup, we would leave and stay overnight with one person or another. I remember one night we spent with the woman who sold Maggi milk; a big black cat came purring onto the bed where my mother and I were lying. Another night I took refuge (without my mother, this time) in the pharmacist's apartment on the ground floor of our building. (I liked her very much. She used to give us big advertising posters to play with, which intrigued and fascinated me.) The next morning she shared breakfast with me on a very pretty tea set and gave me *Gulliver's Travels* as a present.

But our most frequent haven was "the lady on the Rue Labat." She had been my parents' neighbor when they still lived on the Rue des Poissonniers. She had noticed my mother pushing a baby carriage in the street with "such beautiful little blond children," and she always asked after our health. "Now there is a woman who loves children," my mother had said. "She wouldn't let us go without a roof over our heads!"

Leaving our vegetable broth unfinished, and not even quite realizing what the stranger had said, we set out for her house. One Métro stop separates the Rue Ordener from the Rue Labat. Between the two, Rue Marcadet; it seemed endless to me, and I vomited the whole way.

She was home. She was caring for her sister, who had stomach cancer. She agreed to shelter us for a night and offered us Floating Island for dessert. She was wearing a peignoir and looked very lovely to me, and she was so gentle and affectionate that I almost forgot what had brought us to her house that evening.

X

There were seals on the door. They had indeed come. At midnight. Six men from the Gestapo: one for each child. In their anger at coming up empty-handed, they had thrown the furniture out the window, the concierge told us. The armchairs and the sofa from my father's room — everything had been broken, smashed. They'd emptied it out.

Our apartment was on the second floor and opened partly onto a veranda. Thanks to the neighbor who shared our landing and ran a restaurant on the first floor of the building, we were able to enter our "own home" one last time, by the window. Never again, except in dreams, have I ever gone back there. At the end of the war, we were unable to get the apartment back for it had been "occupied," and we were only renting. We were relocated — with other "disaster victims" — on the Impasse Langlois near the Porte de La Chapelle, in an unsanitary slum building without any facilities (in the beginning no electricity, no running water, and revolting outdoor toilets), which served as a refuge for bums and gypsies.

It was supposed to be temporary. It lasted until 1957, when my mother was relocated to a housing project near the Buttes-Chaumont.

We had to move fast. My mother took some photographs, some silverware, and other small items, and then she and I found ourselves on the street again, "wanted," unable to show our yellow star any more without danger, not knowing where to go.

Photo

34

XI

We returned to the Rue Labat. The "lady" agreed to keep us "until we could find a solution." We were practically penniless and had no ration card. Whoever hid us was in danger of being deported or shot, just like us.

She was well liked by all the other tenants in her building, and no one ever betrayed her or us. The neighborhood was full of Jews. Almost every night we were awakened by police cars coming for a raid. "This time it's our turn," we would think. The fear redoubled when the bombing started; then we would have to go down to the cellar in the middle of the night, or into the Métro, and it was impossible to hide our presence from the collaborators in our building.

I still have an especially painful memory of the huge "bombing of La Chapelle." I had had my tonsils removed the day before at an outpatient clinic on the Rue Léon. When the explosions woke us up, I had to be very carefully wrapped in blankets. We stayed in the cellar all night. The next day we went out to see the damage. Almost all the nearby apartment buildings had been destroyed, and the sight of the ruins—only a few

35

sections of wall still standing—made a great impression on me.

This lodging on the Rue Labat was to have been temporary. It lasted throughout the whole war. There was a fresh attempt at the beginning to put me somewhere safer. The "lady" proposed to hide me with the priests on the Rue Notre-Dame-des-Champs. It was true I would have to be baptized, but the baptism could always be annulled after the war. She managed to convince my mother. We three presented ourselves one fine morning at the Institute of Notre-Dame-de-Sion.

The "lady" had just lost her sister and was in deep mourning. She was dressed in black, and I was struck by her blond hair and the soft melancholy in her blue eyes.

To sell me on her plan, she had given me *The Children's Friend* by Berquin as a present. While she and my mother discussed my case with the Reverend Father Devaux, I was left alone in the parlor. In vain I tried to concentrate on the story of the little greyhound. I had seen Father Devaux as we arrived: long red beard, big belly, surplice. He had frightened me, and I was overcome with a strange malaise. I vaguely felt that this time something more was at stake than a separation from my mother.

The door is open, I flee. Nine years old, and I am on the street alone. I decide to take the Métro and return to the Rue Labat. "I've lost my mother," I declare to the ticket taker, and she lets me by without a ticket. I get off at Marcadet-Poissonniers; no one has asked me the slightest question. I climb up the five flights of stairs, trembling, and wait by the door, perched on a step: they'll have to come back sometime! Indeed they did, quite late, and worried, to put it mildly.

The lady decided to keep me.

XII

The apartment had three rooms and a balcony overlooking the street: a small kitchen; no wash-room; the bathroom was on the landing. A stove fueled by wood and coal (harder and harder to get) heated the entire house. There we three had to live together in extremely close quarters until the end of the war. The nicest room, which had been her son's before his marriage, was given to my mother. I slept on a sofa in the bedroom off to the side that served as a dining room. The adjoining room was that of our protectress, the woman who henceforth asked me to call her Mémé, while she christened me Suzanne because that was the saint's name closest to hers (Claire) on the calendar. At first I stayed with my mother. In "her" bedroom I spent my time reading children's books, which I took from the son's glass-fronted bookcase; I also entertained myself by spinning and studying the globe that served as a lamp-shade. I ate kosher food prepared by my mother, who went out from time to time, taking her life in her hands, to see if replenishments could still be found.

But very soon Mémé declared that the food of my childhood was unhealthy; I was pale, "lymphatic," I must change my diet. From then on it was she who would take care of me. Besides, my mother could scarcely ever go out, and I could not do without fresh air. Children were rarely asked for their papers; I could pass for her daughter.

Mémé was a widow, and after her son's marriage and her sister's death, she lived alone, in a state that might be called neurasthenic. Having hoped to be a singer and abandoned her ambitions for health reasons, she ran a little press. Her friend Paul, who had a bookstore on the Rue de Flandre, came over about once a week to have dinner and spend the night with her.

She took great care with her clothes and make-up on those days. She had me set the table with the best damask cloth and the nicest silverware and sent me off to my mother for the evening and the night.

My mother found this state of affairs harder and harder to tolerate; she considered it to be unhealthy but of course could say nothing. It was especially hard for her to endure Mémé's tenderness toward me; she thought it excessive. She knew very well that this woman adored children (she was indeed keeping another little girl during the daytime—Jeanine, of whom I quickly grew jealous), and that she also took in stray cats to feed and pet, but still! Why did she kiss me so often? In the morning, at bedtime, on the slightest pretext! And to be sure, at home we had never gone in for ritual morning and bedtime kisses or such a lot of hugging and commotion.

Bit by bit Mémé brought about a real transformation in me. She changed my hair. My two sisters, whom I envied, wore their hair long and curled in the English fashion. My mother had had mine cut quite short, like a boy's, for I had caught lice at school. I remember the sessions when she washed my scalp with kerosene and went over it with a fine-toothed comb, all the while trying to distract me with a windup puppet that frightened me as much as dolls' eyes and masks did.

My hair grew out but did not curl. Mémé made me two little coils on the top of my head and added a pretty black velvet ribbon. She also revamped my wardrobe: I had been quite poorly dressed, in clothes from mutual aid organizations. Mémé made me clothes to order. She taught me to cut down old garments with a razor blade, and on her sewing machine she made me flared skirts out of the used fabrics, as well as shirred blouses with ruching, and a little coat.

I had to get used to a new diet. Red meat had always been forbidden. On the Rue Ordener my mother let pieces of salted beef drip in the kitchen for hours at a time and then boiled them. On the Rue Labat I had to "restore my health" by eating raw horsemeat in broth. I had to eat pork and "acquire a taste" for food cooked in lard.

I vomited frequently, and Mémé would get angry. I couldn't even swallow the lactose tablets she gave me to improve my digestion. My body was rejecting this foreign diet that was so unfamiliar to me and so unwelcome. Yet she was an excellent cook. In spite of the rationing, thanks to the black market and to the packages of eggs and butter that a cousin sent regularly from Saint-Lô, she managed to prepare delicate little dishes, and I had never eaten so "well." She had me sift the "indigestible" barley flour, which was "liable to give you scabies," through an old silk stocking, so we had sweet white bread for breakfast every day of the Occupation.

After the Normandy invasion the packages stopped coming, and the last months of the war were less idyllic. We had to be satisfied with the soup kitchen, bowls of noodles and beans.

Food and digestive problems were her constant worry. She could detect the tiniest quiver of discontent from her "tube" or mine. She taught me the meaning of *borborygmus* and many other erudite words. The medical dictionary was always close at hand on the dining table. I was allowed to page through it and was transfixed by the illustrated plates of different illnesses and monstrosities; I was especially impressed by the pictures of Siamese twins.

When I was sick, Mémé, unlike my mother, never showed any sign of panic. After being put to sleep with a vial of chloroform, I wake up in the clinic where my tonsils have been removed; both women are at my bedside. I weep and cry out from pain. My mother proceeds to talk very loudly, sympathizing with me in Yiddish, anxious to alert the doctor. Mémé, very calm and smiling, says, "It's nothing terrible! And besides, you'll get a lot of ice to suck on!" Immediately I stop crying. On that day I feel vaguely that I am detaching myself from my mother and becoming more and more attached to the other woman.

XIII

Mother's Day: I take the money out of my "safe" and go out all by myself to the Rue Custine to buy presents for both women: a hairnet and a comb, I think. I also get two postcards. One of them shows a woman's face all smiles, the other a woman seated with a little boy standing at her side. I hesitate a moment, and then I choose the first for Mémé. Of the two, it is the one I find more beautiful. I'm ashamed and feel myself blushing right there in the shop. My choice has undeniably just been made, my preference declared.

A few years earlier Marshal Pétain had organized a contest in the schools: the object was to write the most beautiful letter on the occasion of Mother's Day, a new national holiday he had just instituted. I was one of the winners, and I received an illustrated copy of *The Grasshopper and the Ant*. I had to read my letter aloud in every classroom of the school and show the prize I'd been awarded by the man who was restoring work, family, and fatherland to their place of honor.

XIV

Knowingly or not, Mémé had brought off a tour de force: right under my mother's nose, she'd managed to detach me from her. And also from Judaism. She had saved us, but she was not without anti-Semitic prejudices. She taught me that I had a Jewish nose and made me feel the little bump that was the sign of it. She also said, "Jewish food is bad for the health; the Jews crucified our savior, Jesus Christ; they are all stingy and love only money; they are very intelligent, no other people has as many geniuses in music and philosophy." Then she'd cite Spinoza, Bergson, Einstein, Marx. It is from her lips and in that context that I first heard those names, which are so familiar to me today.

She never stopped repeating that I'd been badly brought up: I obeyed ridiculous religious prohibitions but had no moral principles. I wasn't allowed to say this or do that; this was good, that was bad. She undertook to reform me from head to toe and to complete my education. She made up dictation exercises for me and had me learn *The Cat, the Weasel, and the Bunny Rabbit* by heart. She badgered me about my difficulties with long division: I who was so intelligent, I must be doing it wrong on purpose. She punished me by going out for a walk with Jeanine and leaving me at home alone. It was a well-crafted punishment. She knew perfectly well that my greatest pleasure was to do errands with her, to hear her pass me off as her daughter to the salespeople, and to carry bottles of beer back to the apartment.

Left alone, I sulked in my corner and reverted to sucking my thumb. I could stay that way for long stretches at a time, prostrate, refusing to speak or eat.

Crosswords were one of her favorite pastimes. With her *Larousse* dictionary in hand, I soon got very good at them too. And we would also listen to "great music" all the time. She introduced me to Beethoven—her passion. The radio was always on. I can still see her tapping on it to eliminate static. We used to stay up very late to listen to the English and receive their messages, which she tried to interpret. " 'The dahlias are in bloom,' I repeat 'the dahlias are in bloom.' " And she'd exclaim: "Tonight there'll be a raid, you'll see!" I didn't know whether to admire her perspicacity or her humor, for she liked to laugh and tell funny stories; and she enjoyed cabaret singers.

I didn't have time to feel gloomy or think too much about my mother in the next room, hardly participating in our life at all. She only got me back late on the nights that Paul came, for very soon I took to sharing dinner with Mémé and her friend. I felt awkward on those evenings, though: I didn't quite recognize my everyday Mémé, and I had to be particularly polite at table.

A big framed photograph of General de Gaulle hung over the buffet. He was the great man who was going to save France. When the Allied invasion occurred, Mémé bought a map and pinned a small flag on it for each town that was freed. The day Paris was liberated, we went on foot all the way to the Champs-Élysées, and a man lifted me onto the handlebars of a bicycle so I could catch sight of the general.

Before that, in order to earn a little money, she wove (?) rope nets for civil defense, and I helped her by passing the shuttle back and forth.

XV

I met her whole family: there were some of them I was not supposed to bother because they took a dim view of the little Jewish girl and her mother whom their relative was hiding at great risk to herself. When they came to the Rue Labat, my mother and I had to stay closed up in our room and keep quiet. On the other hand, I was allowed to be "seen" by Mémé's niece and goddaughter, H., a science student who often came to lunch. Mémé loved her very much and called her "my Lénot." H. had a sister, L., a schoolteacher; they were the daughters of Mémé's sister, M., who was herself a schoolteacher. This whole family lived in a small house in L'Haÿ-les-Roses, opposite their grandmother C., Mémé's mother, a very old woman with white hair and sweet blue eyes like Mémé's. On Sundays, we would go to L'Haÿ for a family lunch (Mémé's two brothers R. and C., and their wives, M. and S., were often there, but I had very little contact with them). I was intimidated and would hardly speak at all. After the meal they'd leave me alone for hours in a large room where there was an immense bookcase. I remember devouring *Raoul Daubry* there.

We would return quite late in the evening, always loaded down with irises, dahlias, roses, and jars of preserves made from the raspberries and currents that grew in the old grandmother's garden.

At L'Haÿ I discovered what is known as a family and the family spirit. I was surprised that it was possible to gather several generations together. I had never known my grandmothers, my aunts, uncles, or cousins except in photos. They had all (or almost all) died in the Warsaw ghetto. Once a letter my father sent there was returned by the postal service with the indication "house burned down." Then, nothing. Of my father's ten brothers and sisters, only one escaped, for he was living in Yugoslavia. But there he was shot by the Nazis. Because he had married a non-Jew, he had been rejected by everyone in his own family except my father, who between the ages of sixteen and eighteen, I believe, went to live with him for two years before immigrating to France. Later, when he wrote to him from Paris, my father drew our little hands on the letters as signatures. Our aunt, deeply shaken, outraged by the events of the war and her husband's death, converted to Judaism and left to found a moshav in "Israel" with her two children, Hanna and Aaron.

When my sister Rachel visited her there, she was able to retrieve some photos of my father that we didn't have any longer and to see his letters written in Yiddish with the drawings of our hands. We had all forgotten that tender gesture of my father's, and it came back to me then, all of a sudden, that during the entire war I myself had never ceased drawing my hands.

From that period of my father's life, before his marriage, I have only an old worn-out brown photo that still overwhelms me and pierces my heart. He has his arms crossed, and one of his hands is clearly visible. It looks immense to me, like a hand by Kokoschka. I recognize him especially by his smile, by his crinkly eyes behind his glasses. He doesn't have the beard yet or the hat. He doesn't know yet what lies in store for him.

XVI

One Sunday evening we'd lingered longer than usual at L'Haÿ, our arms full of irises. We had just time to catch the last bus back to the Porte d'Italie, but we missed the last Métro.

We had to get home by foot. When we arrived at the Gobelins Métro station, I was completely exhausted, and we still had to get all the way to Marcadet-Poissonniers.

Mémé decided we'd stay overnight in a hotel. I was relieved and at the same time, without knowing why, extremely worried.

We slept in the same bed. Mémé got undressed behind a big mahogany screen, and I, curious, watched from the bed to catch sight of her when she emerged. Back on the Rue Labat, to the amazement and irritation of my mother, she routinely walked around the apartment in pajamas, her chest uncovered, and I was fascinated by her bare breasts.

I have no memory of that night in the hotel, save of that undressing scene behind the mahogany screen.

The next day we took the first Métro. My

mother was waiting, sick with worry, certain we'd been arrested and obviously unable to inquire at the police station.

I had completely forgotten her. I was quite simply happy.

XVII

My mother suffered in silence: no news from my father; no means of visiting my brothers and sisters; no power to prevent Mémé from transforming me, detaching me from herself and from Judaism. I had, it seemed, buried the entire past: I started loving rare steak cooked in butter and parsley. I didn't think at all any more about my father, and I couldn't pronounce a single word in Yiddish despite the fact that I could still understand the language of my childhood perfectly. Now I even dreaded the end of the war!

One day, all the bells of Paris started to ring at once. The next day we went on foot all the way to the Champs-Élysées to see the parade. There was white bread again in the bakeries. No need anymore to sift bran flour or to buy things on the black market. Some women from the apartment building had their heads shaved, and it was quite a surprise to see a tenant who had been collaborating only the day before sporting an armband of the Free French!

It was the liberation of Paris.

And of my mother. She was finally going to be

able to leave the apartment, live again, get all her children back, perhaps see her husband again! She was finally free, but penniless and homeless. She would have had to sue to recover our apartment, which, after being sealed off, was taken over by a collaborationist doctor. And my mother had other things on her mind: first of all, to reclaim me from the woman who wanted to "steal" me on the pretext that my own mother had more than enough to handle with five other children and wasn't looking after my best interests — which were, according to Mémé, not to be raised by my own mother but rather to be brought up by Mémé herself.

My mother felt nothing any more but hate and contempt for the woman who'd saved our lives. Better to go live in a hotel than stay with her a second longer!

It tore me in two. Overnight I had to take leave of the woman I now loved more than my own mother. I had to share my mother's bed in a miserable hotel room on the Rue des Saules, where we warmed up our store-bought meals on a hotplate that burned butane gas. I refused to eat and spent my time crying until my mother consented to let me go back and see Mémé: "One hour a day," she decreed—just to get me accustomed to the separation—"but no more than that!" If I stayed away a minute too long, she would beat me with a strap. Strangely enough, she had thought to bring that strap with her the day we escaped through the window that gave onto the veranda. . . .

I was soon covered with bruises and began to detest my mother. Life at the hotel with her became intolerable. We went to stay for a while with one of her Jewish friends who lived very far from the Rue Labat. My mother was afraid to let me take the Métro alone, and she rescinded my right to see Mémé.

But I eluded her watchful eye and decided to go and to stay with Mémé, who wanted nothing more than to keep me! However, the law required that I return to my mother, and my mother knew it. So she brought a suit against Mémé. The hearing took place before an improvised Free French tribunal in the play yard of a school. Mémé was accused of having tried to "take advantage" of me and of having mistreated my mother. I didn't understand the expression "take advantage," but I was convinced that my mother was lying. I was outraged to see her falsely accuse the woman to whom we owed our lives and whom I loved so much! I in my turn accused my mother, showing the court my thighs covered with bruises, and I succeeded in making everyone feel sorry for me. The Jewish friend who had taken us in and who had heard the worst imaginable stories about what had happened on the Rue Labat was herself scandalized and promptly switched sides. She confirmed that my mother beat me with a strap.

The Free French tribunal decided to entrust me to Mémé.

A few moments later, Mémé and I are in a phone booth, in a little café on the Rue Marcadet. She is holding me by the hand and smiling, and she is calling her friend Paul, "We won. I'm keeping my little girl!"

Without understanding why, I feel a very strange uneasiness: neither triumphant nor completely happy nor altogether secure.

As I left the café my stomach was in a knot. I was afraid. I peered around me in the street as if

I had just committed a crime—as if once again I were "wanted."

I was, in fact. On the fifth floor of the apartment building on the Rue Labat, my mother was waiting on the landing, accompanied by two men. They tore me violently from Mémé and carried me in their arms all the way down to the street. My mother hit me and shouted at me in Yiddish, "I am your mother! I am your mother! I don't care what the court decided, you belong to me!"

I struggled, cried, sobbed. Deep down, I was relieved.

XVIII

For the cover of my first book, *The Childhood of Art,* I chose a Leonardo da Vinci, the famous London cartoon of the *Madonna and Child with St. Anne.* Two women, the Virgin and Saint Anne, each with the same "blissful smile," bend side by side over the infant, Jesus, who is playing with Saint John the Baptist.

Freud: "The picture contains the synthesis of the history of Leonardo's childhood: its details are to be explained by reference to the most personal expressions in Leonardo's life. In his father's house he found not only his kind stepmother, Donna Albiera, but also his grandmother, his father's mother, Mona Lucia, who — so we will assume — was no less tender to him than grandmothers usually are. These circumstances might well suggest to him a picture representing childhood watched over by mother and grandmother. . . . Leonardo's childhood was remarkable in precisely the same way as this picture. He had had two mothers: first his true mother, Caterina, from whom he was torn away when he was between three and five, and then a young and tender stepmother, his father's wife, Donna Albiera. By his

63

combining this fact about his childhood with the one mentioned above (the presence of his mother and grandmother) and by his condensing them into a composite unity, the design of his 'St. Anne' took shape for him. The maternal figure that is further away from the boy—the grandmother—corresponds to the earlier and true mother, Caterina, in its appearance and in its special relation to the boy. The artist seems to have used the blissful smile of St. Anne to disavow and to cloak the envy which the unfortunate woman felt when she was forced to give up her son to her better-born rival, as she had once given up his father as well. . . . When Leonardo was received into his grandfather's house before he had reached the age of five, his young stepmother, Albiera, must certainly have taken his mother's place where his feelings were concerned."

XIX

Hitchcock's film *The Lady Vanishes* is one of my favorites. I have seen it several times, and each time I am seized with the same visceral anguish when the nice little old lady, Miss Froy, seated in the train opposite the sleeping heroine (a young Englishwoman named Iris), vanishes. It is even worse when she is replaced by another woman who passes herself off as the first. And my agony is excruciating when Iris, having left her seat to look throughout the train for the lady who has vanished, returns to her compartment half-convinced by the pseudodoctor from Prague that the blow to the head she received before getting on the train has caused her to have hallucinations (according to the doctor, Miss Froy—the good little old lady—has never been on the train at all, and seated opposite Iris has always been this other woman who, in fact, has been put there in Miss Froy's place by the conspirators). The part that is always unbearable for me is to perceive, all of a sudden, instead of the good maternal face of the old lady (and everything in the film suggests that she represents the good mother: she calls the mountains at the little ski resort baby's bonnets; she always has extra food with her; when there is no longer enough to eat at the inn, she manages to get cheese for the other guests — especially the English ones; on the train she invites Iris to share her "special" tea in the restaurant car; she's concerned about Iris, advises her to sleep; she poses as a governess, a children's music teacher) the face of her replacement (who is wearing the clothes of the good lady, who is really a secret agent for the Intelligence Service and who is at this point in another compartment, bound and gagged by spies). It is a horribly hard, shifty face, and just as one is expecting to see the good lady's sweet, smiling one, there it is instead — menacing and false.

The bad breast in place of the good, the one utterly separate from the other, the one changing into the other.

XX

After the court decision and its undoing, my mother and I took up residence in a hotel again. Absolutely forbidden to return to my Mémé's apartment! But very soon my mother had to go to Nonancourt to get my brothers and sisters back. In fact, she received an urgent summons to settle a number of problems there right away. She didn't know what to do with me and decided to entrust me once again and despite everything to Mémé!

Our reunion was idyllic. We knew we had only a little time together. Despite an undercurrent of anguish, our joy was intense, and during that whole period, about one month, we slept in the same bed, in her room, in order not to be separated at all this time, day or night. I remember especially the first night, when my emotion and excitement were very great. Just to feel so close to her put me into an "odd" state. I was hot, I was thirsty, I was blushing. I kept mum, and really I would have been hard put to say anything about it, since I had no idea what was happening to me.

Since the war was over, I could go back to school on the Rue Doudeauville. I was ecstatic. In spite of a two-year interruption, I was back in the same class with my old friends Olga Trokacheff, Simone Vidal, Geneviève Lablanche. I got perfect scores in everything, and I adored my new teacher, Mademoiselle Bordeaux.

The school was quite far from the Rue Labat; Mémé would come to get me at the end of the day. We would go home on foot, looking in the shop windows and conversing on every subject. Never had I felt so content.

She bought me a set of watercolors I'd been dreaming of for a long time; she gave me a little illustrated *Larousse* dictionary, which we bought at her friend Paul's bookstore, on the Rue de Flandre, along with a collection of stories by Dickens. With her encouragement I longed for a doll or, rather, for a rubber "bather" (I was still terrified of the eyes of other dolls, which my mother used as a threat when we would refuse to eat), and I hesitated for a long time over the choice of this one or that, without ever really managing to make up my mind.

One afternoon, 4:30, the end of the school day, I rush to the exit, I look for Mémé. It isn't she who is waiting for me but sure enough my mother, come to take me back for good. My heart starts to race. It was atrocious. I was not even allowed to go to the Rue Labat to say goodbye.

We left the next day for Nonancourt.

XXI

My mother was counting on the city to provide us with a small apartment and some furniture. While we waited, all seven of us lived in very cramped circumstances at a hospital that was being used as a hospice. The food there was tasteless, and we had to consume it at the hours prescribed by the establishment: very early in the morning and very early in the evening. We were surrounded by old people, sick people, invalids, midgets (I remember one's name was Nénesse): it was dismal.

Fortunately I had school, my classmates, and my teacher Madame Morin, whom I had known at the school before the war. And yet everything very quickly became unbearable for me. I had no means at all of communicating with Mémé. My mother had forbidden me all contact with her, including letters.

Nonetheless, I had to see her again whatever the cost. One fine day, after school, I decide not to go back to the hospital but to hitchhike to Paris and the Rue Labat — back where Mémé lived.

Nine and a half or ten years old, penniless, without papers, I set out on the main highway. A few cars go by without stopping. I am very worried. Finally a truck stops. There are several men in it.

"What are you doing here?" says one of them.

"I've lost my mother. She lives in Paris. Can you drive me back there?"

And I give the name and address of Mémé.

"Get in!"

They sit me in the back of the truck, in the middle of a pile of rubble, and start up.

I think I am "saved." I hadn't expected it to be so easy! So easy to lie, so easy to get people to believe my lies! Only a hundred kilometers separated me from Paris. I had no qualms and considered I'd as much as arrived already.

Six kilometers from where I'd gotten in, the truck stops. What is going on? We are in Saint-Rémy-sur-Eure, in front of the police station! The truck drivers had not been so naïve as to swallow my story. In any event, they'd preferred to check with the police.

I had to wait for a long time in a large room. My heart was beating fit to kill. What am I going to say? What will they do to me?

I tell the truth, and I am driven back to the hospital in Nonancourt between two policemen. My mother welcomes me with shouts and blows. And she shuts me up for several hours (or days?) in the bathroom.

(On the Rue Ordener, when she couldn't get us to stop shouting, crying, or quarreling, she would shut us up in a dark room[1] that served as a storage space, threatening us that "Maredewitchale"[2] would come for us. I pictured that ghostly and terrifying figure as a very old woman who would come to punish me by carrying me far away from home.)

1. I later wrote a short book entitled *Camera obscura* (Paris: Gallilée, 1973).

2. In *Comment s'en sortir?, Cauchemar* (Paris: Gallilée, 1983), I allude to this character from Jewish folklore, whose name derives from the Indo-European root *mer,* from which came all sorts of evocative words for death, and more specifically for slow death — by suffocation or being eaten alive.

XXII

Soon we moved into the two-room apartment assigned by the mayor's office and lived, all seven of us together, in this tiny space. We were on top of one another, sleeping in the same room, two in a bed. I caught scarlet fever and infected my brothers and sisters, except Annette, who had already had it. I can still see us all together in bed, my mother bringing us borage tea to drink. It was a period of respite. I got no more beatings (anyway, I ended up burying the strap in a hole).

I was sick all the time. After scarlet fever I had a pulmonary congestion, which ended up as an abscess on the lung, with a fever of over 102. I had to return to the hospital, this time as a patient. I was placed in a ward where there were mainly old women, who had a hard time putting up with my spitting and coughing day and night. I stayed there two and a half months. At the beginning, the fever made me delirious, and I had body lice. Then my temperature went below normal for two months, and I became so weak that I wasn't allowed to budge from bed. Antibiotics were not yet in use at the time: I was given injections of camphor and eucalyptus; poultices and cupping glasses were applied; and I drank a great deal of sterilized milk.

I was not too unhappy: I was glad not to be with my mother any more, and — thanks to the complicity of the woman who had hidden Annette and who knew all about my situation — glad to receive letters at last from Mémé, who would always send stamps for my return letter, as well as books. And also I had visits: my classmates and Jeannette, who would bring me books from the Nelson series.

I spent my time reading everything anyone brought me, from the *Vermot Almanach* to *Life of the Ants* by Maeterlinck. In a notebook I kept a list of the words I didn't understand and looked up their meanings in the dictionary. I accumulated by this method quite a little repertory, which I learned by heart. I remember writing DOE: *female hare.*

The hospital's laundress, Madame Aubault, became fond of me, and when I could get up, I would go read my book near her in the laundry room. She had a little boy my age, Claude. Later, she would often invite me to her house near the Madeleine for Sunday lunch, and I would play in the garden with her son.

When I was released from the hospital, there was a fair in the village. My legs were very unsteady. I went walking alone among the shooting galleries and the raffles, the dodg'ems, the swings, and the merry-go-rounds. I remember that a fireman on duty noticed me and offered to give me a cart ride.

Home again from the hospital, I went back to school. Only briefly though, since I had fallen sick in April and the end of the school year was approaching. I earned my grade school diploma, and the day of the awards ceremony, I had a part in a little musical play (*Madame Capulet and Her Neighbor from Picardy*). I played the role of Madame Capulet. Madame Aubault got the hospital to lend me some old woman's clothes, and I was a huge success, making everybody laugh with my antics. My mother, very proud, shouted out loud, "That's my daughter! That's my daughter!" I was ashamed.

(At the end of my last year at the Lycée Jules-Ferry, the parents of prize winners were invited to the ceremony. "Forgetting" that she had done her best to make me quit school and work like my brothers and sisters to "bring in money for the household," my mother repeated the same scene when my name was called, while I, on the stage, wished I could disappear underground.)

The hospital had apparently been good for me. When I left, I seemed reconciled with my family, and I thought I'd forgotten Mémé. A year had gone by. My mother was starting to get tired of the country. It was decided that we would go back to Paris. The mayor's office of the 18th arrondissement offered us an apartment for displaced people near the Porte de la Chapelle.

XXIII

I began going back to see Mémé again, usually accompanied by my sister Annette, who understood my recklessness. My mother seemed resigned and let me do as I liked. But very soon she again put me out of reach of the Rue Labat by sending me for nine months along with Annette to a preventorium in Hendaye for children from the Paris hospitals (I had once for a short time been a patient at Children's Hospital). There I could keep up a regular correspondence with Mémé, and I became very attached to one of the nurses, Madame Navailles. When I left, the separation was, as usual, traumatic.

When we came home again, in order to renew our attachment to Judaism, my mother sent us to Moissac to an establishment for children of deportees, whose program was based on scouting and technical instruction. I stayed there, at the Mill, for five years. During the whole first year I refused to participate in religious services and in community life. To be defiant, I would come down for dinner on Friday evening in a smock. Then, bit by bit, I settled down, under the influence of a scout leader I liked very much, Pierre W. R., who — and this was a great privilege — had me eat at his table. I learned to relish the "joys" of scouting and camping, I sang in the chorus and played the flute (until the day I dropped it by accident from my window on the second floor into the Tarn River). I learned Hebrew again, said all the prayers, and respected the three yearly fasts: once again I obeyed all the religious prohibitions of my childhood.

At the same time, I continued to get letters from Mémé secretly, through my teacher.

At the Mill I soon became an exception: instead of going into a technical program at the end of primary school like most of the other students, I was sent to the coeducational academic high school in town. On Saturdays, I skipped services to attend my classes, and I did my homework on that day as usual.

Madame Cohn, the librarian, a remarkable woman,[1] gave me keys so I could work in the library, which was the only room where, by plugging in the electric heater, I could stay warm in winter. The dormitory rooms, which were quite small and held several students each, were not heated. I became more and more absorbed by my studies and my teachers (men, quite young, preparing for the highest of the competitive state teachers' exams, the *agrégation*). I adored the Latin and Greek professor, Monsieur Bardoux, and my math professors, Monsieur Artigues and Monsieur Batmalle. I was a very serious worker, but I also loved to joke. At the end of class I'd sometimes ask riddles such as, "What is bliss for a mathematician? Give up? Eating square roots at Pythagoras's table." And the whole class would burst out laughing.

I made friends quite soon with another student who especially liked me for my humor. I had "skipped" a grade and gotten into the same class as she. At first, since I was poorly prepared and a little behind because of the war, I was the oldest

1. Later, when I read *The Correspondence of Walter Benjamin and Gershom Scholem*, I learned that she had been Benjamin's intimate friend. In a strange way two apparently unconnected eras of my life met.

in my grade, so I did my sports activities with the class ahead of mine. It was in basketball that I first met Monique Delrieu. We would go together to play games in small neighboring towns, and we swiftly became "inseparable." I think back happily on that little high school, where there were palm trees and basketball nets on the playground and where I spent my best times in Moissac.

Monique lent me textbooks, which I learned by heart, because I had no money whatsoever to buy any of my own. I remember getting a practically perfect score for a geography exercise on "The Etesian Winds," about which I understood absolutely nothing. The entire relevant page in the textbook had simply stuck in my memory.

The municipality of Moissac had lent the Mill for a period of ten years. At the end of my second year, the whole establishment moved to Laversine, to a chateau belonging to the Rothschilds. At the high school in Creil, where I was to continue my schooling, they didn't offer Greek. So I had to return to my mother's apartment, on the Impasse Langlois, little suspecting what a hell I'd have to endure there during my two years of preparation for the final secondary school exams, the *baccalauréats,* in miserable material conditions, forcing myself daily to do all my homework so as to qualify to complete high school. Thanks to Mémé, who had explained the situation to my philosophy teacher and to the directress of the Lycée Jules-Ferry, I managed to complete my secondary education after all. I was a day student on scholarship, so I had my lunch at school, but in the evening I paid the price: there were terrible scenes between my mother and me during meals. I often went on hunger strikes, and I would steal sugar on the sly.

My mother would cut off my electricity early in the evening. I remember reading *Roads to Freedom* by Sartre under the sheets with a flashlight.

At the end of those two years, I had lost twelve pounds and given up all forms of religious practice.

Thanks to a full scholarship, I was able to do the traditional two years of course work in preparation for admission to the best state teachers' school, the École Normale Supérieure. During those years I lived in the dormitory for high school girls on the Rue du Docteur-Blanche: there for the first time I had a room of my own.

Mémé had moved to Les Sables-d'Olonne, where I spent a month's vacation with her in the summer. We went for walks on the beach. I told her everything—all about my schoolmates, about my friend Isaure who bought me cheap tickets to the Comédie Française and the movies, and about the hours of discussions we had together on the existence or nonexistence of God, as we perched on the steps of the Luxembourg Gardens with a sandwich for lunch.

As a university student I lived at the Cité Universitaire, in the Deutsch de la Meurthe house. Here another life begins. For several years I cut off all contact with Mémé: I can't stand to hear her talk about the past all the time or to let her keep calling me her "little bunny" or her "little darling."

When, later, I do come back to see her, I always bring a friend.

She died recently, in a hospice in Les Sables. Seriously disabled, half blind, she couldn't do anything anymore except listen to "great music."

On the telephone she'd hum to me various Beethoven melodies she'd heard.

I was unable to attend her funeral. But I know that at her grave the priest recalled how she had saved a little Jewish girl during the war.

In the *Stages* series

The Rushdie Letters: Freedom to Speak, Freedom to Write. Edited by Steve MacDonogh in association with Article 19

Mimologics. By Gérard Genette. Edited and translated by Thaïs Morgan

Playtexts: Ludics in Contemporary Literature. By Warren Motte

New Novel, New Wave, New Politics: Fiction and the Representation of History in Postwar France. By Lynn A. Higgins

Art for Art's Sake and Literary Life: How Politics and Markets Helped Shape the Ideology and Culture of Aestheticism, 1790–1990. By Gene H. Bell-Villada

Semiotic Investigations: Towards an Effective Semiotics. By Alec McHoul

Rue Ordener, Rue Labat. By Sarah Kofman. Translated by Ann Smock

Palimpsests: Literature in the Second Degree. By Gérard Genette. Translated by Channa Newman and Claude Doubinsky

The Mirror of Ideas. By Michel Tournier. Translated by Jonathan F. Krell

Jacob, Menahem, and Mimoun: A Family Epic. By Marcel Bénabou. Translated by Steven Rendall. Introduction by Warren Motte

Fascism's Return: Scandal, Revision, and Ideology Since 1980. Edited by Richard J. Golsan